Laws of

THE WIT & WISDOM
of GENERAL GEORGE S.
PATTON

Compiled by
CHARLIE "T" JONES
Honorary Member, Tenth Armored Tiger Division

**Executive
Books**

Laws of Leadership Series, Volume VI

The Wit & Wisdom of General George S. Patton

Published by
Executive Books
206 West Allen Street
Mechanicsburg, PA 17055
717-766-9499   800-233-2665
Fax: 717-766-6565
www.ExecutiveBooks.com

ISBN-13: 978-1-933715-55-1

ISBN-10: 1-933715-55-3

Book Production Services
Provided by Gregory A. Dixon

Printed in the United States of America

Table of Contents

Introduction

General George Smith Patton, Jr. was born November 11, 1885 in San Gabriel, California. As a youngster, Patton frequently heard captivating stories of how his ancestors had fought bravely in the Revolutionary, Mexican, and Civil War. The inspired Patton was well on his way to following in the footsteps of his ancestors when he graduated from the United States Military Academy at West Point June 11, 1909.

After graduation, he was assigned to Second Lieutenant in the 15th calvary regiment, and he married Beatrice Ayer on May 26, 1910. In 1912, Patton represented the United States at the Stockholm Olympics in the first Modern Pentathlon.

As a military leader, his high standard of excellence in training his troops made him one of the most outstanding United States field commanders in war situations. In 1917, Patton became the first member of the newly established United States Tank Corps.

After WWI, Patton held a variety of staff jobs in Hawaii and Washington, D.C., and he eventually completed his military training as a distinguished graduate of the Army War College in 1932.

After the attack on Pearl Harbor, the United States entered World War II in December 1941. Patton was commanding the Western Task Force in 1942 and he also commanded the Seventh Army during the invasion of Sicily in July 1943. Patton was given command of the Third Army in France in 1944, and by the time WWII was over, the Third army had liberated 81,522 square miles of territory.

In October 1945, General Patton was placed in charge of the Fifteenth Army in American-occupied Germany. He died on December 21, 1945 after suffering injuries in an automobile accident. His litany of military accomplishments and his ability to lead soldiers to victory has made George S. Patton one of the greatest military leaders in history.

From the
SOLDIER'S TESTAMENT

Written During World War I

It is our duty to judge ourselves
more severely than men judge us.
whatever men say of you,
always remain serene and unangered.
Seen in the quiet mind,
those words which fly so wildly
will only bear their just weight.
Evil hours should be passed
in the silence of Gethsemane.
Turn your eyes upon Me
and do not fret yourself
about the judgments of the world,
for your peace of mind
is not at the mercy of the tongues of men.
Whatever they may think of you,
you can be nothing but what you are,
and where can abide peace, truth and glory
if not in Me?

EVERY

AMERICAN SOLDIER

is a

FOUR-STAR ARMY.

General George S. Patton

Letter to his son, on D-Day, June 6, 1944

By Gen. George S. Patton, Jr. 1885-1945
Commander, Third Army, World War II

Dear George:

At 07.00 this morning the B.B.C. announced...the landing of Allied paratroopers...So that is it.

This group of unconquerable heroes, whom I command, are not yet in, but we will be soon—I wish I were there now as it is a lovely sunny day for a battle...

I have no immediate idea of being killed, but one can never tell and none of us can live forever. So if I should go don't worry, but set yourself to do better than I have.

All men are timid on entering a fight, whether it is the first fight or the last fight...Cowards are those who let their timidity get the better of their manhood. There are apparently two types of successful soldiers—those who get on by being unobtrusive and those who get on by being obtrusive. I am of the latter type and seem to be rare and unpopular, but it is my method. One has to choose a method and stick by it. People who are not themselves are nobody.

To be a successful soldier you must know history. Read it objectively—dates and even minute details of tactics are useless. What you must know is how man reacts. Weapons change, but man, who uses them, changes not at all. To win battles you do not beat weapons—you beat the soul of enemy man...

You must read biography and autobiography. If you will do that you will find that war is simple. Decide what will hurt the enemy the most within the limits of your capabilities and then do it. Take calculated risks. That is quite different from being rash. My personal belief is that if you have a 50% chance you should take it, because the superior fighting qualities of American soldiers will surely give you the extra 1% necessary...

You cannot make war safely, but no dead general has ever been criticized, so you have that way out always. I am sure that if every leader who goes into battle will promise himself that he will come out either a conqueror or a corpse, he is sure to win....Defeat is due not to losses but to the destruction of the souls of the leaders. The "live to fight another day" doctrine.

The most vital quality a soldier can possess is self-confidence, utter, complete, and bumptious. You can have doubts about your good looks, about your intelligence, about your self-control, but to win in war you must have no doubts about your ability as a soldier.

What success I have had results from the fact that I have always been certain that my military reactions were correct. Many people do not agree with me; they are wrong. The unerring jury of history, written long after both of us are dead, will prove me correct.

Soldiers, in fact all men, are natural hero worshipers; officers with a flair for command realize this and emphasize in their conduct, dress, and deportment the qualities they seek to produce in their men....The troops I have commanded have always been well dressed, been smart saluters, been prompt and bold in action, because I have personally set the example in these qualities. The influence one man can have on thousands is a never-ending source of wonder to me. You are always on parade. Officers who, through laziness or a foolish desire to be popular, fail to enforce discipline and the proper wearing of equipment, not in the presence of the enemy, will also fail in battle; and if they fail in battle they are potential murderers. There is no such thing as "a good field soldier." You are either a good soldier or a bad soldier.

Well, this has been quite a sermon; but don't get the idea that it is my swan song, because it is not. I have not finished my job yet.

Your affectionate father, George S. Patton, Jr.

LEADERSHIP

We are in a long war against a tough enemy. We must train millions of men to be soldiers! We must make them tough in mind and body, and they must be trained to kill. As officers we will give leadership in becoming tough physically and mentally. Every man in this command will be able to run a mile in fifteen minutes with a full military pack including a rifle!

I mean every man of this command! Every officer and enlisted man—staff and command; every man will run a mile! We will start running from this point in exactly thirty minutes! I will lead!

****

A leader is a man who can adapt principles to circumstances.

****

You young lieutenants have to realize that your platoon is like a piece of spaghetti. You can't push it. You've got to get out in front and pull it.

****

The most important task of every

Commander does not make any difference what the rank is for promotion. Could be for a colonel or corporal. Picking the right leader is the most important task of every commander. When I have a promotion to make, I line up all of the candidates and give them a problem I want them to solve. I say, "Men, I want a trench dug behind a warehouse. Make this trench eight feet long, three feet wide, and six inches deep." That's all I tell them. I use some warehouse that has windows or a large knot hole. While the candidates are checking out the tools they want to use, I get inside the building and watch through the window or knot hole. The men will drop all of the spades and picks on the ground behind the warehouse as I watch. After resting for several minutes, they will start talking about why I want such a shallow trench. They will argue that six inches is not deep enough for a gun emplacement. Others will argue that such a trench should be dug with power equipment. Others will say it is too hot or too cold to dig. If the men are officers there will be complaints that they should not be doing such lowly labor as digging a trench.

Finally, one man will give an order to the

others, "Let's get this trench dug and get out of here. Doesn't make any difference what that old SOB wants to do with the trench." That man gets the promotion. Never pick a man because he slobbers all over you with kind words. Too many commanders pick dummies to serve on their staff. Such dummies don't know how to do anything except say, "Yes." Such men are not leaders. Any man who picks a dummy cannot be a leader. Pick the man that can get the job done!

****

Generals must never show doubt, discouragement, or fatigue.

****

In cold weather, General Officers must be careful not to appear to dress more warmly than the men.

****

I want you to know that I do not judge the efficiency of an officer by the calluses on his butt.

****

All officers, and particularly General Officers, must be vitally interested in everything that interests the soldier. Usually you will gain a great deal of knowledge by being interested, but even if you do not, the fact that you appear interested has a very high morale influence on the soldier.

****

I prefer a loyal staff officer to a brilliant one.

****

Remember that your primary mission as a leader is to see with your own eyes and to be seen by the troops when engaged in personal reconnaissance.

****

But you need good enemies as much as you need good friends. Having the right enemies is more important than having the right friends. Get the right enemies, and you will have the right friends! You always know where your enemies are. Can never be sure about friends. Sad but true, only a few friends will always be loyal. These lukewarm friends cause people to say, "Protect me from my friends; I can take care of my enemies!" God knows we have enough of these lukewarm friends in the service same as in civilian life. Try to get these types to stand for something. Make them put up or shut up. A great number of military officers I know have never stood for anything other than a short arm inspection! We can differ with each other and still be friends. You will not be my friend if you fail to level with me always.

****

I have enemies, and I want them to stay enemies. They could never be a loyal friend to anything or anybody. I strike at them every chance I can get. It is far better to lose battles with true friends than to win with the enemy. You do not lose a battle when you fight with true friends because you will always be fighting again for the same things. There is no victory when you win with an enemy. That's the reason I have never liked politics and politicians. They are always switching sides—changing bed partners in their politics.

****

There is a great deal of talk about loyalty from the bottom to the top. Loyalty from the top down is even more necessary and much less prevalent.

****

Staff officers of inharmonious disposition, irrespective of their ability, must be removed. A staff cannot function properly unless it is a united family.

****

During the course of this war I have received promotion and decorations far above and beyond my individual merit. You have won them: I as your representative wear them. The one honor which is mine and mine alone is that of having commanded such an incomparable group of Americans, the record of whose fortitude, audacity and valor will endure as long as history lasts.

****

On March 6, 1944, in a Letter of Instruction to his corps, division, and separate unit commanders, Patton wrote:

Full Duty

Each, in his appropriate sphere, will lead in person. Any commander who fails to obtain his objective, and who is not dead or severely wounded, has not done his full duty.

Visits to front

The Commanding General or his Chief of Staff (never both at once) and one member of each of the General Staff sections, the Signal, Medical, ordinance, Engineer, and

Quartermaster sections, should visit the front daily...The function of these...officers is to observe, not to meddle. In addition to their own specialty, they must observe and report anything of military importance. Remember that praise is more valuable than blame. Remember, too, that your primary mission as a leader is to see with your own eyes and be seen by your troops while engaged in personal reconnaissance.

Officers are responsible, not only for the conduct of their men in battle, but also for their health and contentment when not fighting. An officer must be the last man to take shelter from fire, and the first to move forward. Similarly, he must be the last man to look after his own comfort at the close of a march. He must see that his men are cared for. The officer must constantly interest himself in the rations of the men. He should know his men so well that any sign of sickness or nervous strain will be apparent to him, and he can take such action as may be necessary.

So many battles are fought in war and in civilian life, and nothing is gained by the victory. Every battle we fight will result in a gain for us or we will not fight...There is no great gain in merely being right. To be right about some unimportant subject is not important.

****

When we are not moving, we are losing. Nothing ever stays the same in war. We must always be making changes so the enemy will have no idea what we are going to do! We must be able to change our plans every hour and on any hour of the day or night!

****

We herd sheep, we drive cattle, we lead people. Lead me, follow me, or get out of my way.

****

Never tell people how to do things. Tell them what to do and they will surprise you with their ingenuity.

****

You're never beaten until you admit it.

****

It is only by doing things others have not that one can advance.

****

Be willing to make decisions. That's the most important quality in a good leader.

****

If I do my full duty, the rest will take care of itself.

****

Always do everything you ask of those you command.

****

Every man is expendable, including generals, if the results are worth it!

****

When you make a mistake in war, the punishment is death! The trouble is your mistake could cause hundreds of soldiers to die. In war, the enemy does not give a warning before they shoot! That's not the way war works. If the enemy sees you first, he shoots first!

****

When we go into combat I will shoot any man that removes the insignia of our organization or the insignia of his rank. Some generals demand that every man remove all insignia so if captured, the enemy cannot tell what organization they were fighting. We want the enemy to know they are facing the toughest fighting men in the world! ... We are the best and don't ever forget it! For every officer of any rank, non-com or commissioned, I want his rank showing on his helmet. Let that rank be seen! When the officers are leading the men, the enemy knows they are facing a fighting organization and not a group of men being pushed from behind. Any army with the officers in the rear have all of the fighting strength of a bushel of spaghetti being pushed up a hill. Enemy troops will surrender when they see our officers up front! Another thing. Don't worry about being captured. You can be sure you will be treated kindly when you are wearing the insignia of our organization. You tell [them] that if they know what is good for them, they had better surrender because I will never be far away.

****

Our society in 1940 did not train commanders. We trained followers, not leaders. We had the gifted child program. We had the honors programs for gifted children who could secure high grades from their teachers. We taught our children that it was terrible not to have high grades. Our children were smarter than their teachers. The children learned that high grades were necessary for admission to college so the students echoed the words of their teachers. They took more courses where it would be easy to get high grades. They exerted effort for high grades and not for knowledge. After a generation of this training, we had a generation of children who had accumulated high grades but could not face the battles of life—the fear of failure and death. I remember a young man who was a gifted child in grade school. In high school he discovered girls, and the high school teachers discovered that his "gifts" were not as high as his grade school grades. When he received his first high school grades, he was average! This could not be tolerated by his parents. Neither he nor his parents could take the failure of being average. The young man was placed in a private school where he would be protected from being average. This young man has never recovered from his fear of being average. He could not take failure! He could not face any enemy. He was not ready for the battle of life and death.

****

Congress is usually void of leadership. I

don't know that Congress will ever have any leadership because they are always running for reelection. But don't worry about Congress. Just remember we have to live with them. Trying to get reelected every two years breeds great jumpers and not great leaders. Congressman and senators are quick to jump on a horse and ride off in a direction they think the people might be going. If a congressman jumps on a horse going in the wrong direction, he will change horses in a hurry and try to jump at the head of the parade going in some other direction. Great leaders will always lead. A great leader will never try to jump up to the head of a convoy of troops or even public citizens.

****

I don't know what a Philadelphia lawyer might say, but I know what I mean by Country. It is the Constitution! 'Just the greatest document ever written by man' according to an English Prime Minister. You know why we serve the Constitution? Simple! Recall what you said when you got your first commission or got a promotion. You take an oath to God 'to support the Constitution against all enemies foreign and domestic.' We are fighting for our great Constitution. We are not fighting for any man, president, senator, congressman nor potentate. This is what I mean by Country. When you get mad at some Senator or Congressman remember Benedict Arnold. He lost faith in the future of our Country. Of course, the Constitution was not written until several years after Benedict Arnold lost faith in our Country. If he had bounced off the bottom better, he would have been one of our greatest American Generals. He could not take the critics who were angry for his success!

GOD & THE BIBLE

God is truth, and don't ever forget it!

****

Revenge belongs to God. We do not try to get revenge against anybody to get our supplies. Get on the phone and make Washington move! If we cannot get our supplies, we will go with what we've got. If we go out of our way for revenge, we may never get our supplies. Revenge belongs to God!

****

God does not fail at anything. Fear and faith grow together. If you do not have the faith to face death, not much chance you will have enough faith to live a full life. Many of us live half alive and half dead. No beauty in that!

****

Remember in the Bible about the sick man who was told by Jesus to pick up his bed and walk? That sick man did get up and walk away! Pain is just like any enemy. You keep moving around and the enemy cannot hit you. Same way with pain. The quicker you break away from the pain, the quicker you will drive the pain out of your system. You sit too long and you will not be able to move.

****

Never cast your pearls among swine! If the battle is worth it, we will go in and win. If not, we are not going to get shot at without a reason. The Bible tells us not to waste our best on pigs. We are not going into any pig shoot-out! We will kill the enemy where he can be killed easily with the least amount of risk to us. We will not fight the battle the enemy wants us to fight. We will fight on our terms, and we will win always.

****

You get too many fears, you have to find the faith to match the fears. You get too much faith, and you will get more fears to test your faith. God keeps trying to build us up to conquer all fears including death. He never gives us more fears than we can conquer, though. If we give up and fall down with our fears, somehow He will pick us up and give us enough faith to match our fears. If we never give up we can destroy all of our fears.

****

These pulpit killers that go around saying

that the Bible says that man dare not kill causes the death of many thousands of good soldiers. ... little those pulpit killers know about the Bible. They know even less about the way God works. They should read all of the Bible, not just the part they like. God never hesitated to kill. God never hesitates to kill when one man or any race of man needed to be punished. God helped David kill Goliath, didn't he? How about Noah and the Ark? All of the rest of the people were killed in the flood! God took the blame for this mass murder. How about the Red Sea which opened up long enough for one race to escape and another race to be killed. Don't talk to me about God not permitting man to kill. War means that we have to kill people. That's all there is to it. It is not a sin to kill if we are serving on God's side. There is no other way to win. Wars must be won for God's sake. He has a part in every war! The quicker we can kill the enemy, the quicker we can go home and listen to the pulpit killers tell us what we did wrong. If it wasn't for us, those pulpit idiots would be shot for standing in their own pulpits. Our task is to kill the enemy before we are killed.

Soldier & Sailors Prayer

By General George S. Patton

God of our Fathers, who by land and sea has ever led us to victory, please continue your inspiring guidance in this the greatest of our conflicts. Strengthen my soul so that the weakest instinct of self-preservation, which besets all of us in battle, shall not bind me to my duty to my own manhood, to the glory of my calling, and to my responsibility to my fellow soldiers. Grant to our armed forces that disciplined valor and mutual confidence which insures success in war. Let me not morn for those who have died fighting, but rather let me be glad that such heroes have lived. If it be my lot to die, let me do so with courage and honor in a manner which will bring the greatest harm to the enemy, and please, oh Lord, protect and guide those I shall leave behind. Give us the victory, Lord."

CONVICTION & DECISION

I can tell a commander by the way he speaks. He does not have to swear as much as I do, but he has to speak so that no one will refuse to follow his order. Certain words will make you sound like a staff officer and not a commander. A good commander will never express an opinion! A commander knows! No one cares what your opinion is! Never use the words, "In my opinion, I believe, I think or I guess," and never say ""I don't think!" Every man who hears you speak must know what you want. You can be wrong, but never be in doubt when you speak! Any doubt or fear in your voice and the troops can feel it. Another thing. Never give a command in a sitting position unless you are on a horse or on top of a tank!

****

It takes the right mixture of common horse sense and stupidity to make a good commander.

****

Success in war depends upon the golden rule of war. Speed—simplicity—boldness

****

[General Omar] Bradley called up to ask me how soon I could go on the defensive. I told him I was the oldest leader in age and in combat experience in the United States Army in Europe, and that if I had to go on the defensive I would ask to be relieved. He stated I owed too much to the troops and would have to stay on. I replied that a great deal was owed to me, and unless I could continue attacking I would have to be relieved.

****

A General Officer who will invariably assume the responsibility for failure, whether he deserves it or not, and invariably give the credit for success to others, whether they deserve it or not, will achieve outstanding success. In any case, letters of commendation and General Orders presenting to the command the glory and magnitude of their achievements have a great influence on morale.

****

We must always know exactly what we know and what we do not know. Never get the two confused! If we get confused over what we know we can cause many men to die.

****

The best way to issue orders is by word of mouth from one general to the next. Failing this, telephone conversation which should be recorded at each end. However, in order to have a confirmatory memorandum of all oral orders given, a short written order should always be made out, not necessarily at the time of issuing the order, so that, if he has forgotten anything, he will be reminded of it, and, further, in order that he may be aware that his senior has taken definite responsibility for the operation ordered orally.

It is my opinion that Army orders should not exceed a page and a half of typewritten text and it was my practice not to issue orders longer than this.

****

The great things a man does appear to be great only after they are done. When they're at hand, they are normal decisions and are done without knowledge of their greatness.

****

We never assume anything is average. If we do any assuming, we will assume the worst weather.

****

There is a right time to make every decision. Trying to find the right time is the most important factor for all decisions. It is a mistake to make a decision too late. The biggest mistake is to never make a decision! Every old maid agrees with me!

****

When a decision has to be made, make it. There is no totally right time for anything.

****

Some day bemused students will try to see how we came to this decision and credit us with profound thought we never had. The thing as I see it is to get a definite, simple plan quickly, and win by execution and careful detailed study of the tactical operation of lesser units. Execution is the thing, that and leadership.

****

There is no perfect time for anything. We will do what has to be done, and we will do it now! Prompt action immediately on a wrong decision may be far better than the right decision made days later.

****

No man can do anything without knowing what

he is doing. Let the American soldier know what he is fighting for and why. When we let him know what has to be done, he will do it!

****

You may not get killed; only shot! You may collect a bit of lead which could cause a hole that might improve the circulation of your system! For that Washington will give you an award, the Purple Heart! Get hit three times and you could get three medals to wear. Get enough medals and it will make you stronger just to wear them around!

****

Life is like a roller-coaster. Life has its ups and downs. I've been up and down many times. Every time I get an award or win a victory, I expect to be shot at by enemies—even by friends.

****

If everyone is thinking alike, someone isn't thinking.

****

A pint of sweat will save a gallon of blood.

****

A good plan violently executed right now is far better than a perfect plan executed next week.

****

No decision is difficult to make if you get all the facts.

COURAGE & FEAR

Fear is like taking a cold shower. When the water is ice cold, leap in and spread the pain around.

****

There is a time to take counsel of fear, and there is a time to forget your fears. It is always important to know exactly what you are doing. The time to take counsel of your fears is before you make an important battle decision. That is the time to listen to every fear you can imagine! When you have collected all of the facts and fears, make your decision. After you make your decision, forget all of your fears and go full steam ahead.

****

If we take the generally accepted definition of bravery as a quality which knows not fear, I have never seen a brave man.

****

You give me ten good men not afraid to die, and we will destroy an enemy division of ten thousand. That is, if the ten men will stay awake.

****

All men are timid on entering any fight. Whether it is the first or the last fight, all of us are timid. Cowards are those who let their timidity get the better of their manhood.

****

Courage is fear holding on a minute longer.

****

Moral courage is the most valuable and usually the most absent characteristic in men.

****

Take calculated risks. That is quite different from being rash.

****

Go forward until the last round is fired and the last drop of gas is expended...then go forward on foot!

****

Better to fight for something than live for nothing.

****

The coward is the one who lets his fear overcome his sense of duty. Duty is the essence of manhood.

****

Any man who starts thinking he is indispensable will start staying away from the fighting at the front. He will spend more time in the rear eschelons thinking he is too important to risk going where the shells are falling and men are being killed. This man is a coward twice over. He is afraid of himself and of the enemy. In war every man is expendable.

****

Pride in self starts with pride in appearance.

****

Do not be afraid to fail. Never take counsel of your fears.

****

We will need good commanders. It is difficult to train good commanders. A man is either a commander or he is not. We must have men who can lead men into battle. In the history of the world there have been few commanders. It takes the right mixture of common horse sense and stupidity to make a commander. Smart men know that any battle plan can fail. If I had any good sense, for example, I would not be in the army. But ... we've got a war to win. If we don't kill the enemy, they will kill us. It takes a lot of courage to lead men into battles where they can be killed. A commander does not dare to have any fears. If a commander shows any fear, the men can tell. When there is fear of failure, there will be failure.

DISCIPLINE

One must choose a system and stick to it.

****

Discipline is based on pride in the profession of arms, on meticulous attention to details, and on mutual respect and confidence. Discipline must be a habit so ingrained that it is stronger than the excitement of battle or fear of death.

****

There has been, and is now, a great deal of talk about discipline; but few people, in or out of the Army, know what it is or why it is necessary.

****

Every officer and every man must think for himself and be thinking every second. I want my orders followed to the letter after we decide on a battle plan, but I do not want any man around me who 'just does not think.' We may have different ideas, but we will settle on a battle plan. When we settle on a plan, that is the plan we will use. Not because I order it but because it is the best plan based on cold hard facts.

****

You cannot be disciplined in great things and undisciplined in small things. Brave undisciplined men have no chance against the discipline and valour of other men.

****

I am a soldier, I fight where I am told, and I win where I fight.

****

You need to overcome the tug of people against you as you reach for high goals.

****

Always do more than is required of you.

****

Pressure makes diamonds.

****

Colonel…you are removed from command immediately. You hear me? If you know what is good for you, you will stay away from me for a week!

All that "save the ego" nonsense is not for leadership in war. A dead man does not have any ego! How long after you touch a burning match does it take before you get burned? You get your punishment instantly by touching the match. That is the way Mother Nature works, and that's the way war works. What happens to the tree that does not put down its roots? Such a tree will die for lack of water or blow over with the first strong wind. Every mistake has its own punishment. How long does it take for a garden rake to hit you in the face when you step on the teeth turned toward you? Didn't you ever stub your toe on a rock? How long after your toe hits the rock does it take for you to feel the pain?

…What happens when you touch hot electric wires?

You get shocked.

Right! How long after you touch the electric wires until you get this shock?

The shock would come instantly

Right again! Now that time span from the touch and the shock is exactly what we try to do with our training for war. A mistake in war can cause instant death for hundreds of men! We are training for war, colonel. We cannot delay instant death! There is no point in trying to save the ego of a man if the man is dead! War is a killing business!"

Since we have a little time today, let me explain why harsh punishment is so important.

In truth, war is the result of an undisciplined society—a society of people that will not face the truth of discipline. War is a discipline for all of us! Let's get this into our heads. Discipline is a law of Nature! Discipline can be delayed, but it can never be avoided. Mother Nature never lets a wrong go unpunished. The punishment may be years later, and punishment delayed may be more severe. Take parents and kids. If the parents cannot spank the kids, the punishment will be given later by the school teachers. Could be in school the other kids will spank the kids that need punishment. The bottom was cushioned for spanking. God and mother nature never make any mistakes. If these mean kids are not spanked by the teachers in school, they may be put in jail by the police. What happens when we get so many mean kids that the police cannot spank the kids? Self-punishment! Self-punishment is the worst type and the most sever. The kid who cannot discipline himself becomes the man who cannot control his eating and drinking—or his use of drugs. What's the punishment? Liver failure, all kinds of heart problems, lung cancer, and many other severe punishments are given by Mother Nature and God. Could be years later. The saddest part about discipline is that war is the result of a bunch of people who are afraid to spank their kids or put criminals in jail. School is a discipline of the mind. First thing you know, unspanked kids will start insulting their parents and teachers, throwing stones at the school, writing on the walls of public buildings. Why not? There is no punishment! In truth the kids are mad that their parents and the school do not discipline them. Next step is these kids refuse to go into the Army even when drafted. They burn the flag! Or run to Canada. They picket and protest and get little punishment. They might even picket Congress!

We could blame the German people, but we are not free from blame. We bury the discipline of our laws when our leaders break the law without any fear of punishment. Don't always blame the kids. They follow their leaders. Our political leaders and movie stars admit in public to bribery, adultery, bigamy and many major crimes. And the general public approves! Young people follow the examples set by their leaders. Adults are amazed at the violent crimes of the kids as they applaud the violent crimes committed in the movies. Violence by killing is public entertainment in the movies. Can we be amazed when our kids beat up on older citizens?

There is no possible way that any of us can avoid the punishment of Mother Nature. A group of young men at a university in England recently said that they would never give their lives for their country. What happens? The prime Minister of England starts saying, "We want peace in our time! What was he really saying? He is saying he is afraid to die. He is afraid to go to war! What's the result? Some tin horn spoiled kid, such as Hitler, thinks he can whip any country where all of the people want peace. What results? War! When did the war start? In the minds of the men who were shouting for peace at any price! Church ministers climb into their pulpits and preach fear of war! What they are saying is that they are afraid to die. It is impossible to preach fear and a faith at the same time from the same pulpit! Christ said we would always have wars. That is the law of Nature! In the United States we never go to war. We invite the enemy to attack! Colonel, do you understand that war is a result of a basic law of nature? Would you try to brush away a tornado with the back of your hand? Then do not expect me to fail to punish instantly when you make a mistake because in war mistakes can take more lives than a tornado! I cannot kill a man in our combat training, but I can make every man wish to be dead rather than face the wrath of my anger!

There is only one kind of discipline, perfect discipline which gives the punishment at the same instant the mistake is made. When we do not maintain discipline we can cause hundreds to be killed. Christ said, *There will always be wars and rumors of wars.* I wish Christ had told us how to avoid war!

HEALTH

Infantry troops can attack continuously for sixty hours. Frequently much time and suffering are saved if they will do so. Beyond sixty hours, it is rather a waste of time, as the men become too fatigued from lack of sleep.

****

Trenchfoot was becoming very acute at this time. . . . A good deal of the fault was due to the officers and non-coms not taking corrective measures. I wrote a personal letter on trenchfoot and the situation improved.

****

In wet weather it is vital that dry socks come up for the soldiers daily with rations.

****

Staff personnel, commissioned and enlisted, who do not rest, do not last. All sections must run a daily roster and enforce compliance. The intensity of Staff operations during battle is periodic. At the Army and Corps levels the busiest times are the periods from one to three hours after daylight, and from three to five hours after dark. In the lower echelons and in the administrative and supply Staffs, the time of the periods is different, but just as definite. When the need arises, everyone must work all the time, but these emergencies are not frequent: unfatigued men last longer and work harder at high pressure.

****

You got to drive the body to the last inch of energy and then go on! You gain nothing by just going up to where your body says you are tired and exhausted. The body will build and grow only to fit the demands which the mind makes upon the lazy body. If all you do is exercise until the body is tired, the body will get lazy and stop a bit shorter every time. You have to go to the point of exhaustion and go on. That way the body will figure out, "We got to build up more body strength if that crazy mind is going to drive this hard." If you always quit when you are merely tired, you will never gain. Once you let the body tell the mind when to quit, you are whipped for sure. You cannot gain by listening to the body. We can become much stronger if we drive the body. We use about one-tenth of the available strength of our bodies and less than that of our minds!

****

An active mind cannot exist in an inactive body. Always make the mind command the body. To gain strength, always go beyond exhaustion.

****

Now if you are going to win any battle you have to do one thing. You have to make the mind run the body. Never let the body tell the mind what to do. The body is always ready to give up and quit. It is always tired; morning, noon and night. The body is not tired if the mind is not tired.

****

Every muscle which is not used will start to decline in strength within a few hours after use...We can always take one more step! When we are on the attack we can always go one more mile.

SUCCESS

The test of success is not what you do when you're on top. Success is how high you bounce when you hit bottom.

****

We will win because we will never lose! There can never be defeat if a man refuses to accept defeat. Wars are lost in the mind before they are lost on the ground. No nation was ever defeated until the people were willing to accept defeat.

****

You are not beaten until you admit it. Hense don't.

****

In our great Country, most any fool can be a success at something. Look at the flagpole climbers and goldfish eaters! The problem with success is that it leads to failure. When you are on top there is no place to go but down.

****

Accept the challenges so that you can feel the exhilaration of victory.

****

Wars may be fought with weapons, but they are won by men.

****

Make your plans to fit the circumstances.

****

It is the unconquerable nature of man and not the nature of the weapon he uses that ensures victory.

****

Prepare for the unknown by studying how others in the past have coped with the unforeseeable and the unpredictable.

****

I do not fear failure. I only fear the "slowing up" of the engine inside of me which is pounding, saying, "Keep going, someone must be on top, why not you?"

LETTERS

By George S. Patton

My Ambition
(Dated March 1908)

I am fool enough to think that I am one of those who may teach the world its value...Now that is a rash thing to say and if twenty years from now with no war and no promotion some one should say "I thought you were going to teach the world?" why it would hurt. But if there were no dreamers I honestly think there would be little advance and even dreams may, no must come true if a man gives his life for what he believes. Of course it is hard for any one particularly for me who have never done much to give reasons why he believes in my self but foolish as it seems I do believe in my self. I know that if there is war "which God grant" I will make a name or at worst an end... [perhaps] it is only the folly of a boy dreamer who has so long lived in a world of imaginary battles that they only seem real and every thing else unreal...is it not better for a person to stick to the profession he has always thought about than for him to do something for which he has no particular desire or capacity and I certainly have none for any thing but the army. I have thought about it so long that all the other parts of ambition are dead.

****

To My Wife Beatrice
(Dated May 20, 1918)

Darling Beat:

I am leaving this letter with Capt Viner who will send it to you if he feels well assured I have been killed if I am not you will never see it. Of course if I am reported killed I may still have been Captured so don't be too worried.

I have not the least premonition that I am going to be hurt and feel foolish writing you this letter but perhaps if the thing happened you would like it...Beatrice there is no advice I can give you and nothing that I could suggest that you would not know better than I. Few men can be so fortunate as to have such a wife.

All my property is yours though it is not much. My sword is yours also my pistol the silver one. I will give [the horses] Sylvia to Gen. Pershing and Simalarity to Viner.

I think that if you should fall in love you should marry again I would approve...The only regret I have in our marriage is that it was not sooner and that I was mean to you at first...It is futile to tell you how much I love you. Words are as inadequate as is love for a person like you.

If I go I trust that it will be in a manner such as to be worthy of you and of my ideals.

Kiss Beatrice Jr and Ruth Ellen for me and tell them that I love them very much and that I know they will be good.

Beat I love you infinitely,
George

****

Written after World War I in October 1919

We are like the people in a boat floating down the beautiful river of fictitious prosperity and thinking that the moaning of the none too distant waterfall—which is going to engulf us—is but the song of the wind in the trees. We disregard the lessons of History...and we go on regardless of the VITAL necessity of trained patriotism—HIRING an army. Some day it too will strike and then the end. FINIS written in letters of Blood on the map of North America. Even the most enlightened of our politicians are blind and mad with self delusion. They believe what they wish may occur not what history teaches will happen...squeamishness is fatal to any race.

****

Memoir for my deceased father
(Dated July 9, 1927)

Oh! darling Papa I never called you that in life as both of us were too self contained but you were and are my darling. I have often thought that life for me was too easy but the loss of you has gone far to even my count with those whom before I have pitied. God grant that you see and appreciate my very piteous attempt to show here your lovely life. I never did much for you and you did all for me. Accept this as a slight offering of what I would have done.

****

Letter to my deceased mother
(Dated November 30, 1931)

Children are cruel things. Forgive me. I had always prayed to show my love by doing something famous for you, to justify what you called me when I got back from France, "My hero son." Perhaps I still may, but time grows short. I am 46. In a few moments we will bury the ashes of Aunt Nannie. All the three who I loved and who loved me so much are now gone. But you know that I still love you and in the presence of your soul I feel very new and very young and helpless even as I must have been 46 years ago...I have no other memories of you but love and devotion. It is so sad that we must grow old and separate. When we meet again I hope you will be lenient for my frailties. In most things I have been worthy. Perhaps this is foolish but I think you understand. I loved and love you very much. Your devoted son G.S. Patton. Jr.

Charlie "Tremendous" Jones (pictured right) is an Honorary Member of the Tenth Armored Tiger Division. Charlie Jones is also the Founder of Executive Books and the author of the two million copy bestselling book entitled *Life is Tremendous*. The inspiration he received from studying the principles of Patton inspired him to compile *The Wit & Wisdom of General George S. Patton*.

Tenth Armored Division Association

presents an

Honorary Membership

to

Charles "Tremendous" Jones

in recognition of

DISTINGUISHED SERVICE TO OUR MEMBERS

September 6, 1987
<small>Date</small>

Thomas F. Bubin
<small>President</small>

James W. Bierce
<small>Secretary</small>

59

RECOMMENDED READING
Leadership Classics

Patriot's Handbook: A Citizenship Primer for a New Generation of Americans by George Grant

Call of Duty: The Sterling Nobility of Robert E. Lee by Steven J Wilkins

Carry A Big Stick: The Uncommon Heroism of Theodore Roosevelt by George Grant

Four-Star Leadership For Leaders by Charlie Jones and R. Manning Ancell

Never Give In: The Extraordinary Character of Winston Churchill by Stephen Mansfield

Keeping Faith: A Father-Son Story About Love and The United States Marine Corps by John Schaeffer

We Were Soldiers Once...and Young by Harold Moore

They Called Him Stonewall: A Life of Lt. General T.J. Jackson, C.S.A by Burke Davis

Brave Decisions: Moral Courage from the Revolutionary War to Desert Storm by Harry J. Maihafer

For God And Country:Four Stories of Courageous Military Chaplains by John Riddle

Grant Takes Command (1863-1865) by Bruce Catton

Wisdom of the Generals: How to Triumph in Business and in Life by William A. Cohen

All Things for Good: The Steadfast Fidelity of Stonewall Jackson by J. Steven Wilkins

Leadership Secrets of Colin Powell by Oren Harari

RECOMMENDED READING
Leadership Classics

Taking the High Ground: Military Stories of Faith by Jeff O'Leary

Winning Under Fire: Turning Stress Into Success the U.S. Army Way by Dale Collie

At Freedom's Table: More than 200 Years of Receipts and Remembrances from Military Wives by Carolyn Quick Tillery

Lead Like Jesus (Paperback): Lessons from the Greatest Leadership Role Model of All Time by Ken Blanchard

Leadership Wisdom of Jesus: Practical Lessons for Today by Charles C. Manz

Discover *Laws of Leadership* that have stood the test of time.

Self-Improvement Through Public Speaking by Orison Swett Marden

Character Building by Booker T. Washington

7 Golden Rules of Milton Hershey by Greg Rothman

The Greatest Thing in the World by Henry Drummond

The Kingship of Self-Control by William George Jordan

The Wit & Wisdom of General George S. Patton Complied by Charlie Jones

Order From:
www.ExecutiveBooks.com
1-800-233-2665